Table of Contents

....

Introduction

~

"The 65 Things"

~

Resources

By no means is this EVERYTHING you need to know about Medicare. These 65 things will give you the information you need so you know what else you should investigate based on your individual situation. Start early! This knowledge will help you avoid making costly mistakes.

If you are like most people getting ready for Medicare, you aren't sure where to begin. The information in this book will put you on the right track. Resources are provided at the end to help you find answers to your specific questions.

There is a section for notes on each page. The topics will lead you to investigate details you need as you begin the process of learning how Medciare will work for you. Record the information you gather here so you have everything you need at your finger tips.

The book developed from repeated questions asked on my website, MedicareAnswersfromConnie.com, and in my insurance practice working with people who were confused about their Medicare. Helping people understand and use their Medicare benefits to their best advantage is my passion. I hope you find this book useful. Feel free to contact me with your questions or to let me know what you think of the book. I love to hear from you!

Connie

Medicare and Medicaid are not the same thing. Medicare is health insurance for people age 65 and older or those under age 65 who have a qualifying disability. Medicaid is for people of any age with very limited resources.

Notes

_____

_____

_____

Remember, Medicare and Medicaid are not the same thing. It is possible, however, to have both. If you are qualified for Medicare by age (65) or disability and have very limited resources, you may be eligible for both Medicare and Medicaid.

Notes

_____

_____

_____

Medicare covers medically necessary inpatient and outpatient medical treatment. Medicare does not cover outpatient prescription drugs or routine vision, dental or hearing services.

Notes

_____

_____

_____

Medicare is made up of 2 Parts. Medicare Part A and Medicare Part B. These 2 Parts are also referred to as Original Medicare.

Notes
_____

_____

_____

In brief, Medicare Part A covers inpatient hospitalization, limited inpatient skilled nursing facility stays, home healthcare, hospice care and blood. Medicare Part B covers doctor services, tests, durable medical equipment and services performed on an outpatient basis. Medicare Part B also covers ambulance transport.

Notes

_____

_____

_____

Everyone who has earned enough work credits, or who qualifies based on a spouse's earned work credits, qualifies for premium-free Medicare Part A at age 65.

Notes

_____

_____

_____

A minimum of 40 work credits is required to qualify for premium-free Medicare Part A at age 65. One credit is earned for each $1,160 (2013) in net earnings, but no more than four credits may be earned per year. You may also qualify under your spouse's or ex-spouse's work credits.

Notes

_____

_____

_____

If you (or your spouse) have not earned enough work credits to qualify for premium-free Medicare Part A by age 65, you may still enroll in Medicare Part A for a premium. The premium varies depending on the number of work credits that have been earned.

Notes

_____

_____

_____

Failing to enroll in Medicare Part A for a premium when you are initially eligible will result in a premium penalty once you do enroll. Verify your eligibility and enrollment status with Social Security at age 65.

Notes

_____

_____

_____

If you enroll in Medicare Part A for a premium, you must also enroll in Medicare Part B.

Notes

_____

_____

_____

You will be enrolled in Medicare Part A automatically if you are receiving Social Security benefits or have signed up to begin receiving Social Security Retirement benefits at age 65. Verify your eligibility and enrollment status with Social Security at age 65.

Notes

_____

_____

_____

If your 65ᵗʰ birthday is in 2013, you are eligible for Medicare at age 65. However, age 65 is not your Social Security Full Retirement Age. Your Social Security full retirement age is 66. You may begin drawing Social Security Retirement benefits as early as age 62. However, drawing your Social Security Retirement benefits prior to age 66 will result in reduced benefits. Delaying Social Security Retirement Benefits to age 70 will result in up to a 32% increase in benefit amount above your age 66 full retirement benefit.

Notes

_____

_____

_____

You may not decline to enroll in Medicare Part
A if you are receiving Social Security Benefits.

Notes

_____

_____

_____

You may contact Social Security 3 months before your 65th birthday to enroll in Medicare Part A if you are not receiving Social Security benefits or have not signed up to begin receiving Social Security Retirement benefits at age 65.

Notes

_____

_____

_____

You are eligible to sign up for Medicare Part B three months before your 65th birthday month and up to 3 months after your 65th birthday month.

Notes

_____

_____

_____

You will be automatically enrolled in Medicare Part B at age 65 if you are receiving Social Security benefits or have signed up to begin receiving Social Security Retirement benefits.

Notes

_____

_____

_____

Contact Social Security about 3 months before your 65th birthday month to learn about signing up for Medicare Part B if you are not receiving Social Security benefits or have not enrolled to begin receiving Social Security Retirement benefits at age 65. No matter what you have decided to do about enrolling in Medicare, it is a good idea to verify your enrollment status with Social Security at age 65.

Notes

_____

_____

_____

If you sign up for Medicare Part B in the 3 months prior to your 65th birthday, your coverage begins on the first day of your birth month. This also applies to Medicare Part A. There is an exception to this!

Notes

_____

_____

_____

If you enroll in Medicare Part B in the 3 months prior to your 65th birthday, and your birth day is the first of the month, your coverage begins on the first day of the month prior to your birthday month. (This is also true for Medicare Part A)

Notes

_____

_____

_____

Everyone has a Medicare Part B premium.

Notes

_____

_____

_____

The Medicare Part B monthly premium is $104.90 for most people in 2013. There are exceptions to this based on income.

Notes

_____

_____

_____

If you earn more than $85,000/year and file single on your income tax or $170,000 filing jointly, your Medicare Part B premium will be more, based on your earnings.

#23

There is extra help available to assist people with low incomes in paying for the Medicare Part B premium.

Notes

_____

_____

_____

If you fail to enroll in Medicare Part B during your initial eligibility period, and do not qualify for an exception, you may only apply for Medicare Part B in January to March of each year. Your Medicare Part B coverage will begin July 1 of that year. Verify your Medicare enrollment status with Social Security at age 65.

Notes

_____

_____

_____

If you fail to enroll in Medicare Part B during your initial eligibility period, there will be a penalty assessed when you do enroll. Generally that penalty is 10% of the premium for every 12 month period you were eligible but failed to enroll.

Notes

_____

_____

_____

If you continue to work after age 65 and are covered by an employer large (20 or more employees) group health plan or if you are covered under your spouse's large group health plan, you are entitled to the same health benefits provided to employees under age 65. You may delay enrollment in Medicare Part B without a penalty so long as you keep the employer group coverage. (This also applies to Medicare Part A as long as you are not receiving Social Security benefits.)

Notes

_____

_____

_____

27

After age 65 and your initial Medicare enrollment period, should you leave or lose qualified employer group health insurance coverage, you will have a new enrollment period for Medicare Part B. (as well as Medicare Part A if you had not yet begun to receive Social Security Retirement benefits).

Notes

You have 8 months to enroll in Medicare Part B
without penalty once you lose or leave
qualified Employer Group Health insurance.

Notes

_____

_____

_____

If at or after age 65 you are covered by a small employer (less than 20 employees) group health plan or are covered under your spouse's small employer group health plan, in most cases, Medicare is PRIMARY (pays first) to your group health plan. Contact your group plan to verify how they work with Medicare. IMPORTANT! Verify your Medicare enrollment status with Social Security at age 65.

Notes

_____

_____

_____

If you are covered under an employer group health plan or employer retiree health plan after age 65, review your plan (large or small employers alike) to compare your cost and coverage under that health plan to the cost and coverage you would have under Medicare. In many cases you will have better coverage at a lower cost with Medicare, a Medicare Supplement and a Medicare Part D Prescription Plan.

Notes

_____

_____

_____

A Medicare Supplement plan and a Medicare Advantage plan ARE NOT the same thing.

Notes

_____

_____

_____

A Medicare Supplement plan works WITH Medicare Part A and B. A Medicare Supplement pays all or a portion (depending on the plan selected) of Medicare approved costs not paid by Medicare.

Notes

_____

_____

_____

Medicare Supplement plans are designated by letters, A-D, F, G, & K-N. Plan A offers the least benefits, Plan F offers the most benefits.

Notes

_____

_____

_____

#34

Medicare Supplement plans are also known as Medigap plans because they fill in some or all of the gaps left by Original Medicare A and B.

Notes

_____

_____

_____

Medicare Supplement plans are regulated by the Federal Government but are not part of the Federal Government. Private insurance companies sell Medicare Supplement plans. Federal guidelines require that Medicare Supplement plan benefits be exactly the same per plan no matter what company sells the Supplement Plan. For example, a Plan F (or any other plan) has the same benefits no matter what company you buy the Plan F (or any other plan) from.

Notes

_____

_____

_____

#36

The Federal Government allows insurance companies to set their own premium for Medicare Supplement plans. Medicare Supplement plan premiums can vary greatly depending on the company you buy the plan from.

Notes

_____

_____

_____

You are guaranteed enrollment in a Medicare Supplement plan, no matter your health conditions, for up to 6 months after your 65th birthday or when you are first enrolled in Medicare Part B.

Notes

_____

_____

_____

A Medicare Supplement plan allows you to see any doctor or use any hospital or facility that accepts Medicare.

Notes

_____

_____

_____

Your Medicare Supplement plan may not be canceled by the insurance company except for your failure to pay the premium. If your Medicare Supplement insurance company goes out of business, you are guaranteed enrollment in a similar plan with another company within 2 months of losing your coverage.

Notes

You may cancel or change a Medicare Supplement plan at any time, but, after your initial guarantee enrollment period for a Medicare Supplement ends, you must go through health underwriting to apply for a Medicare Supplement. You may be declined coverage at this time based on your health conditions. Some states offer additional guaranteed open enrollment periods.

Notes

Many states and insurance companies allow you to apply for a Medicare Supplement up to 6 months prior to your 65th birthday. Find out the rule for your state.

Notes

_____

_____

_____

Remember, Medicare Supplement plans and Medicare Advantage plans are not the same thing. Medicare Advantage plans are also called Medicare Part C. Medicare Advantage plans are not part of the Federal Government (like Original Medicare Parts A and B are). Medicare Advantage plans are private insurance companies that take assignment of and manage the benefits of your Original Medicare Part A and Part B.

Notes

_____

_____

_____

#43

Medicare Advantage plans have networks of hospitals, facilities and doctors which you must use in order to realize the full benefits of the Medicare Advantage plan. Going outside the Advantage plan network, except in emergencies, may result in you being responsible for the entire cost of your treatment.

Notes

_____

_____

_____

You may enroll in a Medicare Advantage plan 3 months prior to and up to 3 months after your 65th birthday month.

Notes
_____

_____

_____

You may cancel a Medicare Advantage plan for any reason within your first 12 months of enrollment (a "FREE LOOK" period) in that Medicare Advantage plan. Canceling in this case also allows you guarantee issue in a Medicare Supplement plan for up to 2 months after leaving the Advantage plan. This only applies to your FIRST enrollment and any subsequent enrollment plan changes are not allowed the 12 month "FREE LOOK" period or guarantee enrollment in a Medicare Supplement.

Notes

_____

_____

_____

#46

You may change Medicare Advantage plans each year during Annual Enrollment which is October 15 to December 7 (2012). Some enrollment period exceptions apply based on residence, income and health conditions. Health underwriting is not required to enroll in a Medicare Advantage plan; however, there are Special Needs plans for certain health conditions.

Notes

_____

_____

_____

You may drop a Medicare Advantage plan and return to Original Medicare January 1st to February 14th each year.

Notes

_____

_____

_____

Medicare Part D is the part of Medicare that covers prescription drugs.

Notes

_____

_____

_____

You may enroll in a Medicare Part D
Prescription drug plan, 3 months prior to your
65th birthday month and up to 3 months after.

Notes
_____

_____

_____

There is a penalty of 1% per month of the previous year's average Medicare Part D premium assessed for every month you go without a Medicare Part D Prescription drug plan past your initial eligibility enrollment period.

Notes

_____

_____

_____

Medicare Part D plans are regulated by the Federal Government but provided by private insurance companies.

Notes

Insurance companies that offer Medicare Part D Prescription drug plans may set their own premiums, copays and deductibles (up to a set maximum) which are approved by the Federal Government according to Medicare Part D guidelines.

Notes

_____

_____

_____

All Medicare Part D plans must be structured the same way: Initial Coverage Level, Coverage Gap, and Catastrophic Coverage Level.

Notes

_____

_____

_____

Some but not all Medicare Part D plans have a deductible that must be met in the initial coverage level. The maximum deductible a Medicare Part D drug plan may have is $325 (2013).

Notes

_____

_____

_____

During the Medicare Part D Initial Coverage Level, you and the insurance company each contribute to the cost of your drugs. You pay the deductible, if any, and any copays for your medications. The insurance company pays the remainder of drug costs.

Notes

_____

_____

_____

When the total cost of your medications, (what you have paid and what the insurance company has paid), reaches $2970 (2013), you enter the Coverage Gap.

Notes

_____

_____

_____

You are responsible for the total cost of your medications once you enter the Medicare Part D Coverage Gap (also known as the Donut Hole). Medications, based on their cost and tier level, are available at up to a 52% discount when you are in the Medicare Part D Coverage Gap.

Notes

_____

_____

_____

EASTER

Salutations

58

When the total cost YOU have paid for your medications, (what <u>only</u> you have paid in the Initial Coverage Level plus what you have paid in the Coverage Gap), reaches $4750 (2013), you enter the Medicare Part D Catastrophic Coverage Level.

Notes

_____

_____

_____

Copays for medications are greatly reduced in the Medicare Part D Catastrophic Coverage Level. You pay 5% of the cost of a medication or $2.65 for generic drugs / $6.60 for all other drugs, whichever is greater.

Notes

_____

_____

_____

Every January 1st you start over in the Medicare Part D Initial Coverage Level regardless of whether you keep the same plan or switch plans. You must meet the plan deductible, if any, and the financial milestones that move you through the 3 levels of coverage for each new year.

Notes

_____

_____

_____

You may change Medicare Part D Prescription drug plans each year during Annual Enrollment, October 15 to December 7 (2012), regardless of your health conditions. The new plan starts January 1st of the following year. Plan benefits tend to change each year. Review your plan before Annual Enrollment ends each year.

Notes

_____

_____

_____

There are Special Election Periods that allow you to make changes to or add a Medicare Part D Prescription drug plan outside annual enrollment or initial enrollment periods if you meet certain criteria. These criteria may include but are not limited to moving outside a plan service area, changes in qualifications for extra help and nursing home resident status. It's a good idea to seek professional advice if you have a change in your life that you feel could affect how you receive benefits.

Notes

_____

_____

_____

If you earn more than $85,000/year filing single, $170,000 filing jointly, your Medicare Part D Prescription drug plan monthly premium will be more, based on your earnings.

Notes

_____

_____

_____

There is extra help available to pay for the Medicare Part D Prescription drug plan premium, deductible and copays for people with low incomes.

Notes

_____

_____

_____

Medicare Part D Prescription drug plans have formularies - the list of drugs a Medicare Part D Prescription drug plan covers. Drugs are assigned tiers in the formulary that specify copay amounts. Plans are required to cover drugs in each medication category that is considered medically necessary but are not required to cover every drug in a particular category. Some of your medications may not be covered by a particular plan. Drugs may be assigned higher tiers on one plan than another. Research before you enroll!

Notes

_____

_____

_____

RESOURCES

Medicare Answers from Connie is your trusted source for simplified, straight answers to your Medicare questions as well as a resource for quotes on Medicare Supplements and Medicare Part D Prescription Drug Plans.
www.MedicareAnswersfromConnie.com
connie@connieulmer.com

Helpful Medicare Publications

These may be found at www.Medicare.gov or contact me by e-mail and I will send you the publication electronically

Medicare and Other Health Benefits: Your Guide to Who Pays First   CMS Publication # 02179

Medicare Coverage of Diabetes Supplies & Services   CMS Publication # 11022

Medicare and You, 2013   CMS Product #10050

RESOURCES

Choosing a Medigap Policy: A Guide to Health
Insurance for People with Medicare
CMS Product #02110

TRICARE For Life Handbook
www.tricare.mil

Medicare   1-800-633-4227

Social Security   1-800-772-1213

Notes

_____

_____

_____

_____

_____

_____

_____

_____

_____

www.ingramcontent.com/pod-product-compliance
Lightning Source LLC
Chambersburg PA
CBHW050811290526
45792CB00001B/70